Rabbit
WARREN
PEACE

A Retelling of
LEO TOLSTOY'S CLASSIC

Rabbit
WARREN
PEACE

BLACK & WHITE PUBLISHING

First published 2016
by Black & White Publishing Ltd
29 Ocean Drive, Edinburgh EH6 6JL

1 3 5 7 9 10 8 6 4 2   16 17 18 19

ISBN: 978 1 78530 058 5

Original work by Leo Tolstoy 1869
Translation and abridgement © Black & White Publishing 2016
Photographs © Black & White Publishing 2016

A CIP catalogue record for this book is available from the British Library.

Photography by Ali Miller
Additional photography by Thomas Ross
Designed and typeset by Henry Steadman
Printed and bound by IMAGO

TOLSTOY & RABBITS

If the rabbits in this book help just a few more people tackle the full, original text of this literary masterpiece, then their work and effort getting all dressed up will have been more than worthwhile. Although rabbits do not feature heavily in the original work – just once in more than half a million words – it is gratifying to see that their existence is noted by Tolstoy.

· · ·

The question of how man's consciousness of freedom is to be reconciled with the law of necessity to which he is subject cannot be solved by comparative physiology and zoology, for in a frog, a rabbit, or an ape, we can observe only the muscular nervous activity, but in man we observe consciousness as well…

from War & Peace by Leo Tolstoy
Second Epilogue, Chapter VIII

DRAMATIS PERSONAE

Natasha Rostova

Princess Maria Bolkonskaya

Prince Vasili Kuragin

Nikolai Rostov

DRAMATIS PERSONAE

Pierre Bezukhov

Anatole Kuragin

Helene Kuragin

Prince Andrei Bolkonsky

Fedya Dolokhov

St Petersburg
July 1805

At Anna Pavlovna Scherer's Reception…

"Well, Prince, so Genoa and Lucca are now just family estates
of the Buonapartes. But I warn you, if you don't tell me that this
means war, if you still try to defend the infamies and horrors
perpetrated by that Antichrist Napoleon — I really believe he is
Antichrist — I will have nothing more to do with you and you
are no longer my friend!"

Anna Pavlovna Scherer's words rang in the ears of Prince Vasili Kuragin — the Emperor Napoleon was out to conquer Europe.

Pierre Bezukhov was one of the next arrivals – a stout, heavily built young man with close-cropped hair, spectacles, the light-coloured breeches fashionable at that time, a very high ruffle, and a brown dress coat. The illegitimate son of Count Bezukhov, this was his first appearance in society. Anna Pavlovna greeted him with the nod she accorded to the lowest hierarchy in her drawing room.

All evening, Pierre was afraid of missing any clever conversation and where it seemed interesting, he stood waiting for an opportunity to express his own views, as young people are fond of doing.

Who would inherit old Count Bezukhov's immense fortune.
Illegitimate Pierre or Prince Vasili Kuragin?

Prince Andrei Bolkonsky was a very handsome young man, of medium height, with firm, clearcut features. Everything about him, from his weary, bored expression to his quiet, measured step, offered a most striking contrast to his quiet, little wife Lise. It was evident that he not only knew everyone in the drawing room, but had found them to be so tiresome that it wearied him to look at or listen to them. And among all these faces that he found so tedious, none seemed to bore him so much as that of his pretty wife. He turned away from her with a grimace that distorted his handsome face.

"You are off to the war, Prince?" said Anna Pavlovna.

"General Kutuzov," said Bolkonsky, speaking French and stressing the last syllable of the general's name like a Frenchman, "has been pleased to take me as an aide-de-camp...."

When he saw Pierre's beaming face, Prince Andrei gave him an unexpectedly kind and pleasant smile.

Prince Vasili's daughter Princess Helene passed between the chairs, lightly holding up the folds of her dress, and the smile shone still more radiantly on her beautiful face. Pierre gazed at her with rapturous, almost frightened, eyes as she passed him.

"Very lovely," said Prince Andrei.

"Very," said Pierre.

Prince Vasili seized Pierre's hand and said to Anna Pavlovna: "Educate this bear for me! He has been staying with me a whole month and this is the first time I have seen him in society. Nothing is so necessary for a young man as the society of clever women."

"Papa, we shall be late," said Princess Helene, turning her beautiful head and looking over her classically moulded shoulder.

It was the name day of two of the Rostovs — the mother and the youngest daughter — both named Natasha. Ever since the morning, carriages with six horses had been coming and going continually, bringing visitors to the Countess Rostova's big house on the Povarskaya, so well known to all Moscow. The countess looked at her callers, smiling affably, but not concealing the fact that she would not be distressed if they now rose and took their leave.

The count jumped up and, swaying from side to side, spread his arms wide and threw them round the little girl who had run in.

"Ah, here she is!" he exclaimed laughing.
"My pet, whose name day it is. My dear pet!"

"Ma chere, there is a time for everything," said the countess with feigned severity. "You spoil her, Ilya," she added, turning to her husband.

This black-eyed, wide-mouthed girl was just at that charming age when a girl is no longer a child, but not yet a young woman.

A carriage containing Pierre (who had been sent for) and Anna Mikhaylovna (who found it necessary to accompany him) was driving into the court of the dying old Count Bezukhov's house.

Prince Vasili and the eldest princess were sitting under the portrait of Catherine the Great and talking eagerly.

"But, my dear," said Prince Vasili suddenly, "what if a letter has been written to the emperor in which the count asks for Pierre's legitimisation? Do you understand that in consideration of the count's services, his request would be granted?... That letter was written, though it was not sent, and the emperor knew of it. The only question is, has it been destroyed or not? If not, Pierre will get everything as the legitimate son."

Soon the princess had the letter in her hand. As Pierre and his companion entered, suddenly Anna Mikhaylovna seized the letter and held it tightly. The deed was done, the intriguers foiled, and Pierre would now be the new Count Bezhukhov, in command of an immense fortune.

I, Count Bezukh...
hereby name as
my sole heir
Pierre Bezukh...

"I know you enough to be sure that this will not turn your head,
but it imposes duties on you, and you must be a man."

As the threat of war with Napoleon loomed ever larger,
young men prepared for battle.

"Well, now, goodbye!" Old Prince Nikolai Bolkonsky gave his
son his hand to kiss, and embraced him. "Remember this,
Prince Andrei, if they kill you it will hurt me, your old father..."
He paused unexpectedly, and then in a querulous voice suddenly
shrieked: "but if I hear that you have not behaved like a son of
Nikolai Bolkonsky, I shall be ashamed!"

"You need not have said that to me, Father," said the son with a smile.
"I also wanted to ask you," continued Prince Andrei, "if I'm killed
and if I have a son, do not let him be taken away from you — as I said
yesterday... let him grow up with you... Please."

"Not let the wife have him?" said the old man, and laughed.

They stood silent, facing one another. The old man's sharp eyes
were fixed straight on his son's. Something twitched in the lower
part of the old prince's face, then he turned and departed.

When Prince Andrei had left for war, the study door opened quickly. "Gone? That's all right!" said the old man and slammed the door.

With Prince Andrei wounded and feared lost following the disastrous
battle of Austerlitz, talk of war consumes Moscow. Napoleon is near at hand.

Nikolai Rostov and Vasili Denisov are home on leave and,
before long, Denisov has fallen in love.

"Mamma!... Mamma!... He has made me..."

"Made what?"

"Made, made me an offer, Mamma! Mamma!" she exclaimed.
Countess Rostov is astonished. Little Natasha was suddenly grown
up and had a decision to make.

"Vasili Denisov, I'm so sorry for you!... No, but you are so nice...
but it won't do... not that... but as a friend, I shall always love you."

Meantime, Nikolai Rostov was having trouble paying off his immense
gambling debts. His father, the Count, was once again very short of money.
Only a good marriage for Nikolai could save them, but Nikolai only
had eyes for penniless Sonya.

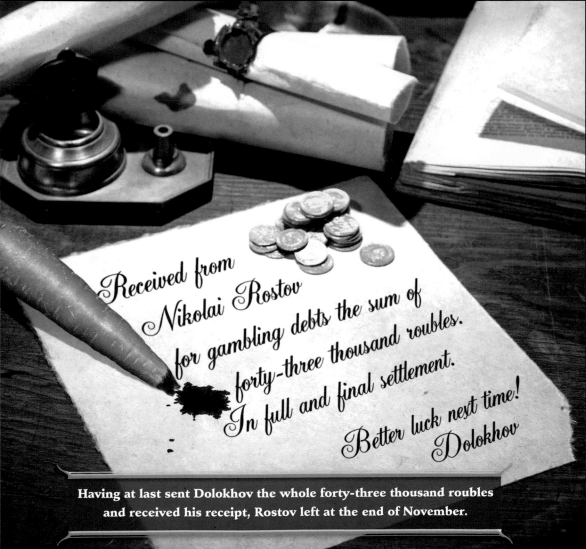

Received from
Nikolai Rostov
for gambling debts the sum of
forty-three thousand roubles.
In full and final settlement.

Better luck next time!
Dolokhov

Having at last sent Dolokhov the whole forty-three thousand roubles and received his receipt, Rostov left at the end of November.

In Moscow, Count Rostov was planning a banquet but the news about Pierre Bezukhov was not good. Pierre had married the beautiful Helene but all was not well. A guest in Pierre's house, Dolokhov had compromised her completely.

Pierre had received an anonymous letter that morning, which in the mean jocular way common to anonymous letters said that he saw badly through his spectacles, but that his wife's connection with Dolokhov was a secret to no one but himself.

He feared now to look at Dolokhov, who was sitting opposite him. Every time he chanced to meet Dolokhov's handsome insolent eyes, Pierre felt something terrible and monstrous rising in his soul and turned quickly away.

"Well, now to the health of handsome women!" said Dolokhov, and with a serious expression, but with a smile lurking at the corners of his mouth, he turned with his glass to Pierre – "and their lovers!" he added.

"You...! you... scoundrel! I challenge you!" Pierre ejaculated, and, pushing back his chair, he rose from the table.

Pierre looked down at his feet, then quickly glanced at Dolokhov and, bending his finger as he had been shown, fired.

Pierre had of late rarely seen his wife alone. Both in Petersburg and in Moscow their house was always full of visitors. The night after the duel he did not go to his bedroom but, as he often did, remained in his father's room, that huge room in which Count Bezukhov had died.

He lay down on the sofa meaning to fall asleep and forget all that had happened to him, but could not do so. Now he seemed to see her in the early days of their marriage, with bare shoulders and a languid, passionate look on her face, and then immediately he saw beside her Dolokhov's handsome, insolent, hard, and mocking face as he had seen it at the banquet, and then that same face pale, quivering, and suffering, as it had been when he reeled and sank on the snow.

"What has happened?" he asked himself. "I have killed her lover, yes, killed my wife's lover. Yes, that was it! And why? How did I come to do it?" — "Because you married her," answered an inner voice. "In marrying her without loving her; in deceiving yourself and her." And he vividly recalled that moment after supper at Prince Vasili's, when he spoke those words he had found so difficult to utter: "I love you." "It all comes from that! Even then I felt it," he thought. "I felt then that it was not so, that I had no right to do it. And so it turns out."

Helene's brother, Anatole, used to come to borrow money from her and used to kiss her naked shoulders. She let herself be kissed.

Two months had elapsed since the news of the battle of Austerlitz and the loss of Prince Andrei had reached Bald Hills, and in spite of the letters sent through the embassy and all the searches made, his body had not been found nor was he on the list of prisoners.

Then, on the day his wife went into labour, Prince Andrei was returned. Suddenly he realised the joyful significance of that wail; tears choked him, and leaning his elbows on the window sill he began to cry, sobbing like a child.

A woman rushed out and seeing Prince Andrei stopped, hesitating on the threshold. He went into his wife's room. She was lying dead, in the same position he had seen her five minutes before and, despite the fixed eyes and the pallor of the cheeks, the same expression was on her charming childlike face with its upper lip covered with tiny black hair.

Five days passed, and then the young
Prince Nicholas Andreevich was baptised.

At the Rostov's, Natasha came running out to Nikolai. "I was looking for you. I told you, but you would not believe it," she said triumphantly. "Dolokhov has proposed to Sonya!"

Little as Nikolai had occupied himself with Sonya of late, something seemed to give way within him at this news.

"And fancy! she refused him quite definitely!" adding, after a pause, "she told him she loved another."

"Yes, my Sonya could not have done otherwise!" thought Nikolai.

"Do you know, Nikolai — don't be angry — but I know you will not marry her. I know, heaven knows how, but I know for certain that you won't marry her."

"But I must talk to her. What a darling Sonya is!" he added with a smile. A minute later Sonya came in with a frightened, guilty, and scared look. Nikolai went up to her and kissed her hand. This was the first time since his return that they had talked alone and about their love.

"I have already refused," she said hurriedly.

Nikolai again kissed Sonya's hand. "You are an angel: I am not worthy of you, but I am afraid of misleading you."

At the Petersburg ball, Prince Andrei, in the uniform of a cavalry colonel, stood looking animated and bright in the front row of the circle not far from the Rostovs. Pierre came up to him and caught him by the arm.

"You always dance. I have a protegee, the young Rostova, here. Ask her," he said.

Approaching Natasha he held out his arm to grasp her waist before he had completed his invitation. He asked her to waltz. That tremulous expression on Natasha's face, prepared either for despair or rapture, suddenly brightened into a happy, grateful, childlike smile.

"I have long been waiting for you," that frightened happy little girl seemed to say by the smile that replaced the threatened tears, as she raised her hand to Prince Andrei's shoulder. They were the second couple to enter the circle. Prince Andrei was one of the best dancers of his day and Natasha danced exquisitely.

Natasha was happier than she had ever been in her life.
She was at the height of bliss.

Next day Prince Andrei called at a few houses he had not visited before, and among them at the Rostovs' with whom he had renewed acquaintance at the ball. Natasha was one of the first to meet him. She was wearing a dark-blue house dress in which Prince Andrei thought her even prettier than in her ball dress.

In Natasha, Prince Andrei was conscious of a strange world completely alien to him and brimful of joys unknown to him. After dinner Natasha, at Prince Andrei's request, went to the clavichord and began singing. Prince Andrei stood by a window talking to the ladies and listened to her. In the midst of a phrase he ceased speaking and suddenly felt tears choking him, a thing he had thought impossible for him. He looked at Natasha as she sang, and something new and joyful stirred in his soul.

Prince Andrei needed his father's consent to his marriage. Old Prince Bolkonsky received his son's communication with external composure, but inward wrath. He could not comprehend how anyone could wish to alter his life or introduce anything new into it, when his own life was already ending.

"I beg you to put it off for a year: go abroad, take a cure, look out as you wanted to for a German tutor for Prince Nicholas. Then if your love or passion or obstinacy — as you please — is still as great, marry! And that's my last word on it. Mind, the last…" concluded the prince, in a tone which showed that nothing would make him alter his decision.

Prince Andrei saw clearly that the old man hoped that his feelings, or his fiancee's, would not stand a year's test, or that he (the old prince himself) would die before then, and he decided to conform to his father's wish — to propose, and postpone the wedding for a year.

Calendar

JANUARY

	1	2	3	4	5	6
7	8	9	10	11	12	13
14	15	16	17	18	19	20
21	22	23	24	25	26	27
28	29	30	31			

FEBRUARY

28	29	30	31	1	2	3
4	5	6	7	8	9	10
11	12	13	14	15	16	17
18	19	20	21	22	23	24
25	26	27	28			

MARCH

25	26	27	28	1	2	3
4	5	6	7	8	9	10
11	12	13	14	15	16	17
18	19	20	21	22	23	24
25	26	27	28	29	30	31

APRIL

1	2	3	4	5	6	7
8	9	10	11	12	13	14
15	16	17	18	19	20	21
22	23	24	25	26	27	28
29	30					

MAY

29	30	1	2	3	4	5
6	7	8	9	10	11	12
13	14	15	16	17	18	19
20	21	22	23	24	25	26
27	28	29	30	31		

JUNE

27	28	29	30	31	1	2
3	4	5	6	7	8	9
10	11	12	13	14	15	16
17	18	19	20	21	22	23
24	25	26	27	28	29	30

JULY

1	2	3	4	5	6	7
8	9	10	11	12	13	14
15	16	17	18	19	20	21
22	23	24	25	26	27	28
29	30	31				

AUGUST

			1	2	3	4
5	6	7	8	9	10	11
12	13	14	15	16	17	18
19	20	21	22	23	24	25
26	27	28	29	30	31	

SEPTEMBER

31	1	2	3	4	5	6
7	8	9	10	11	12	13
14	15	16	17	18	19	20
21	22	23	24	25	26	27
28	29	30				

OCTOBER

28	29	30	1	2	3	4
5	6	7	8	9	10	11
12	13	14	15	16	17	18
19	20	21	22	23	24	25
26	27	28	29	30	31	

NOVEMBER

26	27	28	29	30		1
2	3	4	5	6	7	8
9	10	11	12	13	14	15
16	17	18	19	20	21	22
23	24	25	26	27	28	29

DECEMBER

1	2	3	4	5	6	7
8	9	10	11	12	13	14
15	16	17	18	19	20	21
22	23	24	25	26	27	28
29	30	31				

"But I shall die, waiting a year: it's impossible, it's awful!" Natasha looked into her lover's face and saw in it a look of commiseration.

Nearly a year later, two remarkably pretty girls, Natasha and Sonya, with Count Rostov who had not been seen in Moscow for a long time, attracted general attention. Moreover, everybody knew vaguely of Natasha's engagement to Prince Andrei, and knew that the Rostovs had lived in the country ever since, and all looked with curiosity at a fiancée who was making one of the best matches in Russia.

At the opera, Helene introduced Natasha to her dashing brother Anatole. Natasha turned her pretty little head toward the elegant young officer and smiled at him over her bare shoulder. Anatole, who was as handsome at close quarters as at a distance, sat down beside her and told her he had long wished to have this happiness.

As they were leaving the theatre Anatole came up to them, called their carriage, and helped them in. As he was putting Natasha in he pressed her arm above the elbow. Agitated and flushed she turned round. He was looking at her with glittering eyes.

Only after she had reached home was Natasha able clearly to think over what had happened to her, and suddenly remembering Prince Andrei she was horrified, and at tea to which all had sat down after the opera, she gave a loud exclamation, flushed, and ran out of the room.

"O God! I am lost!" she said to herself. "How could I let him?"

Anatole asked Natasha for a valse and as they danced he pressed her waist and hand and told her that he loved her.

Natasha did not sleep all night. She was tormented by the insoluble question of whether she loved Anatole or Prince Andrei. She loved Prince Andrei — she remembered distinctly how deeply she loved him. But she also loved Anatole, of that there was no doubt, little knowing that he was already married.

But Anatole's elaborate plan to elope with Natasha was betrayed. "Well, it doesn't matter," said Prince Andrei. "Tell Countess Rostova that she was and is perfectly free and that I wish her all that is good."

As Napoleon's army of 400,000 men again threatened Moscow, old Prince Bolkonsky died of a stroke, and the peasants were in revolt. A revolt quelled in part by Nikolai Rostov and his men, gaining him the gratitude and admiration of Bolkonsky's daughter, Princess Maria.

The impression the princess made on Rostov was a very agreeable one. To remember her gave him pleasure. It made him angry just because the idea of marrying the gentle Princess Maria, who was attractive to him and had an enormous fortune, had against his will more than once entered his head.

For himself Nikolai could not wish for a better wife: he would make his mother happy and be able to put his father's affairs in order.

Pierre was handed the broadsheets. The French would enter Moscow. He thought it now a certainty. Overwhelmed, Pierre set off for the front line, at Borodino. As he toured the battlefield, looking for some way to serve his Fatherland, Dolokhov came up to him and took his hand.

"I am very glad to meet you here, Count," he said aloud in a particularly resolute and solemn tone. "On the eve of a day when God alone knows who of us is fated to survive, I am glad of this opportunity to tell you that I regret the misunderstandings that occurred between us and should wish you not to have any ill feeling for me. I beg you to forgive me."

Later, as Prince Andrei prepared for battle, he suddenly looked out and saw Pierre: "You? What a surprise!" said he. "What brings you here?"

"I have come... simply... you know... come... it interests me," said Pierre, "I wish to see the battle."

After the battle, several tens of thousands of the slain lay in diverse postures and various uniforms on the fields and meadows of Borodino. At the dressing stations the grass and earth were soaked with blood for a space of some three acres around.

On the retreat, Pierre hears that both Prince Andrei and his brother-in-law Anatole have fallen in battle.

After dinner the whole Rostov household set to work with enthusiastic haste packing their belongings and preparing for their departure from Moscow.

That night a wounded man was driven down the Povarskaya and brought into the Rostovs' yard. This wounded man was Prince Andrei Bolkonsky.

"Mamma," said Sonya, "Prince Andrei is here, mortally wounded. He is going with us."

The countess opened her eyes in dismay and, seizing Sonya's arm, glanced around. "Natasha?" she murmured.

At that moment this news had only one significance for both of them. They knew their Natasha, and alarm as to what would happen if she heard this news stifled all sympathy for the man they both liked.

"Well, Mamma? Everything is ready. What's the matter?" asked Natasha, as with animated face she ran into the room.

"Nothing," answered the countess. "If everything is ready let us start."

"Look! It's Bezukhov!" said Natasha, putting her head out of the carriage and staring at a stout man in a coachman's long coat.

As the French occupy Moscow, Pierre remains. He is determined to assassinate Napoleon and put an end to Russia's suffering. But his plan fails when he is arrested and imprisoned by French soldiers. Forced to retreat with Napoleon's army in the harsh Russian winter, only a Russian raiding party, led by Denisov and Dolokhov, saves Pierre from an uncertain fate. In the skirmish, however, the youngest Rostov boy, Petya, falls.

For Prince Andrei, his chance meeting with Natasha gave him comfort, and her a chance to make amends.

"Forgive me!" she whispered, raising her head and glancing at him. "Forgive me!"

"I love you," said Prince Andrei.

"Forgive me for what I ha-ve do-ne!" faltered Natasha in a scarcely audible, broken whisper, and began kissing his hand more rapidly, just touching it with her lips.

"I love you more, better than before," said Prince Andrei, lifting her face with his hand so as to look into her eyes.

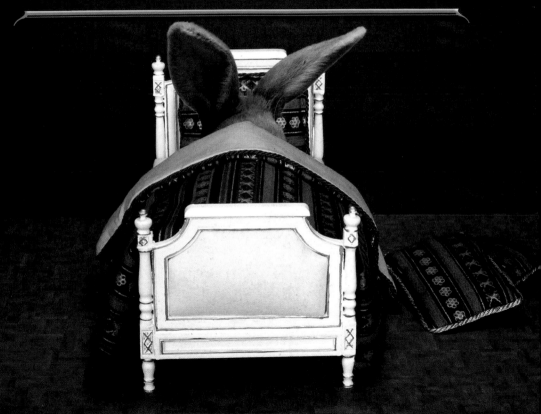

Prince Andrei's last days and hours passed in an ordinary and simple way.

With Prince Andrei and Petya Rostov now dead, Pierre learned by chance of the death of his wife Helene. All this at the time seemed merely strange to Pierre: he felt he could not grasp its significance. Just then he was only anxious to get away as quickly as possible from places where people were killing one another, to some peaceful refuge where he could recover himself, rest, and think over all the strange new facts he had learned.

Pierre decided to visit Princess Maria, who was sitting with her companion. When he mentioned the Rostovs, Princess Maria's face expressed great embarrassment. She again glanced rapidly from Pierre's face to that of the lady in the black dress and said:

"Do you really not recognise her?"

Pierre looked again at the companion's pale, delicate face with its black eyes and peculiar mouth. "But no, it can't be!" he thought.

When she smiled doubt was no longer possible, it was Natasha and he loved her.

"You love him?" asked Princess Maria.

"Yes," whispered Natasha.

Count Ilya Rostov died that same year and, as always happens, after the father's death the family group broke up.

The events of the previous year: the burning of Moscow and the flight from it, the death of Prince Andrei, Natasha's despair, Petya's death, and the old countess' grief fell blow after blow on the old count's head.

He seemed to be unable to understand the meaning of all these events. When Pierre and his wife had left, he grew very quiet and began to complain of depression. A few days later he fell ill and took to his bed. He realised from the first that he would not get up again.

Natasha's wedding to Pierre, which took place in 1813, was the last happy event in the family of the old Rostovs.

The friendship between Nikolai Rostov and Princess Maria had cooled. "But why, Count, why?" she almost cried, unconsciously moving closer to him. "Why? Tell me. You must tell me!"

He was silent.

"I don't understand your why, Count," she continued, "but it's hard for me... I confess it. For some reason you wish to deprive me of our former friendship. And that hurts me." There were tears in her eyes and in her voice. "I have had so little happiness in life that every loss is hard for me to bear... Excuse me, goodbye!" and suddenly she began to cry and was hurrying from the room.

"Princess, for God's sake!" he exclaimed, trying to stop her. "Princess!"

She turned round. For a few seconds they gazed silently into one another's eyes — and what had seemed impossible and remote suddenly became possible, inevitable, and very near.

In the winter of 1813 Nikolai Rostov married Princess Maria
and moved to Bald Hills with his wife, his mother, and Sonya.

Nikolai and his wife lived together so happily that even Sonya and the old countess, who felt jealous and would have liked them to disagree, could find nothing to reproach them with.

Natasha looked joyfully at her husband, Pierre. It was not what he said that pleased her — that did not even interest her, for it seemed to her that was all extremely simple and that she had known it a long time (it seemed so to her because she knew that it sprang from Pierre's whole soul), but it was his animated and enthusiastic appearance that made her glad.

The moment they were alone, Natasha came up to him with wide-open happy eyes, and quickly seizing his head pressed it to her bosom, saying: "Now you are all mine, mine! You won't escape!" The simultaneous discussion of many topics did not prevent a clear understanding but on the contrary was the surest sign that they fully understood one another.

'What nonsense it is about honeymoons being the greatest happiness,' Natasha exclaimed. 'On the contrary, now is best of all!'

If you are interested in getting a rabbit of your own, there are hundreds of rescue centres across the country that could help pair you up with the right furry friend. The RSPCA, the SSPCA and dozens of rabbit rescue centres are the perfect way to find the right rabbit for you. Check online for details.

EAST LINKS FAMILY PARK

The Publishers would like to thank the management and staff at
East Links Family Park, Dunbar, for their help and cooperation
with the photographs in this book. The rabbits at East Links are
extremely well cared for and are used to meeting the general public
and being handled by their regular handlers, who were involved
throughout the photography. East Links Family Park is
open all year (www.eastlinks.co.uk for details) and the rabbits
(and other animals) would love to see you there!

VERY SPECIAL THANKS ALSO TO…
Ruth Bailey for her fabulous costume designs and the beautifully
fitted final costumes, and to Jackie Holt for her invaluable input
at the start of the project. The rabbits loved their new looks and
definitely wanted to keep them, particularly for winter!

And to Henry Steadman, creative genius extraordinaire,
for his design ideas, endless patience and unstinting work.
And for being a top bloke.